Original title:
Yondered Stems Over the Unicorn Mow

Author: Liina Liblikas
ISBN HARDBACK: 978-1-80562-015-0
ISBN PAPERBACK: 978-1-80563-536-9

Canvas of Secrets and Blooms

In the garden where whispers reside,
Petals unfold like secrets untold.
Colors dance in the morning light,
Stories of magic begin to unfold.

Beneath the arch of the ancient oak,
Lies the laughter of shadows unseen.
In the brush of the artist's stroke,
Dreams of a world where hearts can glean.

Every leaf a tale of the past,
Every root a path leading deep.
In the silence, the moments last,
Planting memories we hold and keep.

As twilight drapes its velvet cloak,
The stars begin their gentle sighs.
With each glance, the night awoke,
Painting the skies with whispered lies.

So tread softly on this canvas bright,
With every step, create your spell.
In the garden where dreams take flight,
A tapestry of secrets to tell.

Heartstrings of the Gentle Blades

In the fields where the wildflowers sway,
Gentle breezes hum a sweet refrain.
Each blade of grass a soft ballet,
Dancing lightly, free of chain.

Sunlight drapes in a golden hue,
Caressing hearts with tender grace.
Nature sings in morning dew,
A symphony of time and space.

The whispers twine like lovers' hands,
Binding moments, forever near.
As the landscape softly expands,
So blooms the courage to draw near.

With every rustle, a secret shared,
Each heartbeat echoes in the glade.
The beauty found when ones have cared,
Threads of light that never fade.

So in the dusk where shadows play,
Find comfort in the evening's call.
Heartstrings tug as night holds sway,
Cradling dreams in the starlit thrall.

Whispers of Enchanted Meadows

In meadows lush, where shadows play,
The whispers of the breeze do sway.
Beneath the sky, so vast and blue,
A magic stirs, both old and new.

Where daisies dance and willows weep,
The secrets of the earth do keep.
With every rustle, soft and clear,
A song of love floats near and near.

The lilac blooms in twilight's hue,
Its perfume drapes the evening dew.
And as the fireflies start their flight,
The meadows glow with pure delight.

A tapestry of emerald dreams,
We weave our wishes, hopeful themes.
In the heart of every flower,
Resides a fleeting, fleeting power.

So linger here, let time stand still,
Embrace the magic, feel the thrill.
For in this place of purest heart,
A world of wonder won't depart.

Dance of the Celestial Blossoms

Beneath a moon of silver light,
The blossoms sway, a wondrous sight.
With petals soft as whispered dreams,
They twinkle softly, like sunbeams.

In rhythms sweet, the nightingale,
Sings tales of love on zephyr's trail.
The blossoms twirl, a mystic grace,
In every petal, a sacred space.

The stars above in splendor shine,
As shadows stretch in perfect line.
They dance with joy in starlit skies,
A festivity that never dies.

Where twilight weaves its gentle thread,
The petals whisper tales unsaid.
In every shimmer, every twink,
The bonds of fate begin to link.

So join the dance, let spirits soar,
With every step, we seek for more.
The celestial blossoms call in song,
A harmony where we belong.

Twilight's Ethereal Bloom

As twilight wraps the world in gold,
A softer story begins to unfold.
With every star that pierces dim,
The night takes root, serene and grim.

Among the blooms of shadows deep,
The secrets of the night do keep.
In silken whispers, they impart,
The essence of a dreaming heart.

A fragrant mist surrounds the glade,
In velvet hues, the dusk is laid.
The moonbeams dance on petals rare,
And swirl like fairies through the air.

With every sigh, the twilight sighs,
Revealing truths in soft replies.
For in this magic-laden night,
Hope blooms anew, a guiding light.

So wander where the shadows creep,
And cradle the dreams that time will keep.
For twilight's bloom, in gentle grace,
Awaits the soul's enchanted space.

Serenade of Faerie Fields

In faerie fields where time stands still,
A serenade of joy does fill.
With laughter ringing through the trees,
The magic whispers on the breeze.

The flowers sway, alive with song,
In colors vibrant, pure, and strong.
Each petal holds a tale to tell,
Of dreams that rise, of hearts that swell.

The brook's soft murmur, gentle, clear,
Draws creatures close, both far and near.
With every ripple, secrets flow,
As faeries dance in twilight's glow.

The evening star glimmers with pride,
A sentinel for dreams that bide.
In every corner, joy takes flight,
In faerie fields, beneath the night.

So close your eyes and breathe it in,
The magic calls, let dreams begin.
For in these fields where wonders meet,
The heart's own rhythm finds its beat.

Echoes of a Wandering Heart

In shadows deep, where dreams unfold,
A heart will wander, fierce and bold.
It seeks the light, beyond the night,
In every whisper, hope takes flight.

Through tangled woods and rivers wide,
It longs for truth, with stars as guide.
Each step it takes, a story spun,
A tale of love, not yet begun.

The echoes call, like distant bells,
Of secret paths and hidden spells.
With every heartbeat, journeys start,
Unraveling threads of a wandering heart.

And though the road may twist and bend,
The wanderer's spirit will not end.
For in each shadow, light will gleam,
A promise found in every dream.

So travel on, dear heart so free,
Embrace the magic, let it be.
For in your quest, you'll find your place,
In every smile, a warm embrace.

The Petals' Lullaby to the Stars

In twilight's hush, the petals sway,
They sing to stars at close of day.
With whispers sweet, they softly hum,
A lullaby where dreams do come.

The moonlit glow on dewdrops shine,
Each flower's grace a tale divine.
They cradle secrets, soft and bright,
Inviting wishes into the night.

Oh gentle blooms, so bold and fair,
With every breath, you fill the air.
You teach the heart to find its way,
Through dark to dawn, through night to day.

Listen closely, when shadows creep,
The petals sing, their promise keep.
For in their song, the cosmos twirls,
A dance of dreams, of boys and girls.

So lay your worries with the stars,
And feel the magic that's truly ours.
In every petal, a story flows,
A lullaby where wonder grows.

Portraits of the Wildflower Spring

In fields adorned with colors bright,
The wildflowers dance in pure delight.
Each petal paints a story told,
In hues of red, in shades of gold.

With every breeze, a whisper flows,
Of sunshine days and gentle glows.
They sway and twirl in playful cheer,
The portraits of spring, so crystal clear.

A tapestry of life unfolds,
In every blossom, a dream bolds.
Each fragrant note, a hymn of grace,
Invites the heart to find its place.

The wildflowers sing, a chorus sweet,
For every soul they wish to meet.
Their laughter weaves through air so light,
A promise held in morning's sight.

So wander forth where petals lie,
Beneath the vast and blue-lit sky.
For in their beauty, truth does spring,
In portraits bright, our hearts take wing.

Garden of Lost Moonlight

In shadows deep, the moonlight sighs,
Where dreams reside and whispers rise.
A garden lost, in silver glow,
Holds secrets that the night will know.

Each flower blooms in stillness rare,
With petals kissed by nighttime air.
They hold reflections of the past,
In gentle hues that fade too fast.

The echoes of laughter drift away,
In moonlit gardens where spirits play.
Amid the thorns, a tender heart,
Seeks solace in the quiet art.

Yet in this space, where shadows blend,
A promise waits, a chance to mend.
For every tear that fell like rain,
Brings forth the blooms of hope again.

So stroll the paths where moonlight weaves,
Embrace the night, the heart believes.
In gardens lost, beneath the stars,
Find peace and love, despite the scars.

Forgotten Spirits of the Mowed Meadow

In meadows wide, the whispers call,
Forgotten spirits, where shadows fall.
They dance among the blades so green,
In twilight's glow, they weave unseen.

With laughter light, they sway in air,
With secrets shared, a hidden care.
A flicker here, a shimmer there,
They weave their dreams, a tapestry rare.

Beneath the stars, their voices blend,
In gentle breezes, they transcend.
A waltz of time, a graceful flight,
In mowed meadows, they find their light.

Through fields once known, their echoes roam,
In every breeze, they find their home.
A soft embrace, a lover's sigh,
In the heart of night, they softly cry.

So heed the whispers, soft and sweet,
In mowed meadows, their spirits meet.
Forgotten yet, they sense our glance,
And lure us in, this timeless dance.

Whirls of Color in Forgotten Lands

In lands forgotten, colors swirl,
Where dreams awaken, moments unfurl.
A tapestry woven with hues so bright,
Each step reveals a new delight.

The azure skies and ruby streams,
In shades of wonder, silence gleams.
A canvas kissed by nature's hand,
In every hue, the stories stand.

Whirls of crimson, whispers of gold,
A tapestry of tales untold.
With each soft breeze, the colors play,
In forgotten lands, they find their way.

Among the shadows in rustling leaves,
A world of magic, the heart believes.
With fields of lavender, skies of gray,
In every color, memories stray.

So let us wander through realms so bright,
In whirls of color, find our light.
For in forgotten lands we dare,
To dream anew, to breathe the air.

Beneath the Eloquence of Green

Beneath the trees, where voices hum,
In gentle whispers, nature's drum.
The eloquence of green unfolds,
In every leaf, a tale retold.

The breeze, it carries songs of old,
In verdant chambers, secrets hold.
The sunbeams dance on emerald glade,
While light and shadow serenade.

With every rustle, life rebirths,
In tangled roots, the earth weaves worth.
A symphony of life begins,
Where laughter swells and sorrow thins.

Amidst the ferns, in soft embrace,
We find our peace, a sacred space.
Beneath the eloquence, we remain,
In nature's heart, we feel no pain.

So linger here beneath the green,
In whispered words, truths yet unseen.
For nature's breath will always sing,
In tranquil woods, our souls take wing.

Where Fantasy Roots Within

In lands where dreams and shadows play,
Where whispers cast the night to day.
In secret glades, the magic wakes,
And every heart a pathway takes.

With fireflies dancing, glowing bright,
They guide the wanderers through the night.
Where wishes dwell and sorrows cease,
In fantasy's arms, we find our peace.

In realms adorned with silver sighs,
The tapestry of starlit skies.
With every thought, a portal spins,
In worlds where fantasy roots within.

Amidst the laughter, joy will swell,
In every tale, we weave our spell.
To dream of castles, dragons bold,
In stories lost, yet still retold.

So close your eyes, let visions flow,
Where fantasy whispers, hearts will glow.
For in this realm of wondrous spins,
We find our truth where magic begins.

Whispers of Fantastical Meadows

In meadows where the fairies dance,
The grass wears dew like a soft trance.
Beneath the sky of azure hue,
A magic thread weaves me and you.

The whispers float on gentle air,
Caressing dreams with tender care.
Each blossom tells a tale so sweet,
Where time and wonder gently meet.

The sunbeams kiss the petals bright,
In this realm, all hearts take flight.
With every breeze, new worlds arise,
And secrets twinkle in the skies.

Here shadows play with dappled light,
While creatures bask in pure delight.
A painting brushed by nature's hand,
In this enchanting, golden land.

So wander deep, let spirit soar,
Each footfall leads to worlds galore.
In fantastical meadows vast,
Our dreams entwined, forever cast.

Echoes of Enchanted Blossoms

In gardens rich with vibrant blooms,
Where laughter sings and magic looms.
Petals whisper secrets old,
And tales of love and kin unfold.

The roses blush in twilight's glow,
Where past and present ebb and flow.
Each fragrance weaves a fragrant tale,
As starlit skies begin to pale.

Under arching boughs aglow,
The moonlight casts a silver show.
With every rustle, each soft sigh,
The heart finds solace wandering by.

In every bud, a story sleeps,
Of laughter light, of dreaming leaps.
The echoes of enchanted grace,
Invite the wonders to embrace.

Though seasons change and time moves on,
The essence of these blooms stays strong.
In every petal, joy resounds,
In enchanted gardens, love abounds.

Shadows Beneath Celestial Horns

Beneath the stars with silver crowns,
Where whispered dreams in twilight drown.
The shadows stretch, and night confides,
In hidden paths where magic hides.

Among the trees with gnarled limbs,
The moonlight dances; the night sings hymns.
A tapestry of dark and light,
Unraveled glory, shimmering bright.

With every rustle, secrets spill,
From thickets deep, the air grows still.
The celestial horns begin to play,
As shadows whirl and softly sway.

Each whisper calls from depths of night,
Guiding all who seek the light.
Through realms unknown, they softly tread,
In search of wonders yet unsaid.

So linger not in mundane lands,
For dreams await with open hands.
Shadows beneath the stars proclaim,
A world alive, a wild flame.

Treading the Dreamscape of Flora

In the dreamscape where whispers bloom,
Each petal sways, dispelling gloom.
With every step through gardens rare,
A tapestry of colors flare.

Where rivers hum a gentle tune,
And sunbeams dance with soft monsoon.
The flora beckons, vibrant, free,
In this realm of mystery.

Among the shadows, sunlight weaves,
Where magic rests upon the leaves.
In dreams that twine like ivy's cling,
An orchestra of wonders sing.

Each breath reveals a tale unspun,
As day and night in twilight run.
In every blossom's radiant smile,
The heart discovers joy worthwhile.

So tread with care on paths of light,
For dreams await the bold and bright.
In the dreamscape, flora guides,
To realms where every heart abides.

A Symphony of Serene Buds

In the garden, dreams take flight,
Whispers of fragrance soft and light,
Every petal sways with grace,
Nature hums in a tranquil space.

Sunbeams dance on morning dew,
Colors bloom in vibrant hue,
Harmony in each flower's sigh,
A melody where spirits lie.

Gentle breezes brush the leaves,
Nature's quilt, the heart believes,
Each bud tells a secret tale,
Swaying softly in the gale.

Underneath the azure sky,
Hope unfurls, and dreams comply,
With every note, a tender thrum,
In the symphony, hearts succumb.

From the roots to lofty boughs,
The world sings softly, all it vows,
In celebration, life abounds,
In the garden, joy surrounds.

Wanderlust in the Wildflower Tongue

In meadows wide where dreams ignite,
The wildflowers giggle, pure delight,
Their petals dance on the whims of breeze,
Whispering tales through the swaying trees.

A wanderlust flows, sweet and bold,
In hues of sunshine, stories told,
Each flower speaks in colors bright,
Inviting souls to take their flight.

With heartbeats matched to nature's song,
A path is woven, winding, long,
Through fields of laughter, freedom's grace,
In wildflower tongues, we find our place.

The earth beneath, a cradle soft,
Revealing secrets, aloft, aloft,
As we run through blooms, hearts in bloom,
Wanderlust beckons, dispelling gloom.

So let us roam in playful glee,
Where petals beckon, wild and free,
In nature's arms, we lose our way,
Yet find ourselves, come what may.

Beneath the Glistening Canopy

Beneath the trees, a world of dreams,
Where sunlight spills in golden beams,
Leaves chatter soft in secret tones,
As ancient roots weave tales in stones.

The forest breathes a fragrant sigh,
With shadows dancing, low and sly,
Each twig and leaf a mystery,
Whispering wild, enchanting history.

Beneath the glistening canopy,
Life pulses rich in harmony,
The rustle calls to hearts so bright,
In tangled depths, we find our light.

Ferns unfurl, a gentle sway,
In sunlight's kiss, they find their way,
Each moment cradled, soft and sweet,
A haven where the wild souls meet.

So linger long beneath the boughs,
In nature's grip, embrace the vows,
For in the stillness, we may find,
The whispering truths that bind our kind.

Reality's Canvas of Blossoms

Upon the canvas, colors burst,
In every bloom, a moment's thirst,
Each stroke a story, rich and bold,
Crafted in petals, warmth untold.

Reality blurs where dreams entwine,
With blossoms bright, a fate divine,
Every fragrance, a memory spun,
In a dance of life, we become one.

Brushes dipped in shades of grace,
Paint the world, a gentle place,
With laughter echoing in the air,
Artistry blooms, vibrant and rare.

In twilight's glow, the colors blend,
Crafting shadows that softly mend,
A masterpiece where hearts belong,
In reality's weave, a tender song.

So let us bloom, our spirits soar,
On life's canvas, forevermore,
For in each bloom, a dream takes flight,
Painting the world with pure delight.

Tides of Color Over Hidden Valleys

Beneath the sky so wide and bright,
A dance of colors takes its flight.
The valleys whisper tales untold,
In hues of crimson, orange, gold.

Where shadows play and rivers gleam,
A tapestry of nature's dream.
The lilies sway in gentle grace,
While breezes weave a warm embrace.

And as the sun begins to set,
A symphony of light is met.
The valleys sing in tones so clear,
In every shade, a voice we hear.

Through rustling leaves, the secrets flow,
In painted skies, where wishes grow.
For every dawn that breaks anew,
Unfolds the magic, rich in hue.

So heed the call of nature's art,
Let colors dance within your heart.
Embrace each stroke, let visions thrive,
In hidden valleys, we feel alive.

The Harp of Nature's Serenade

In twilight's glow, a whisper plays,
A harp that weaves through sunlit days.
With every breeze, a note ascends,
The chorus of the earth transcends.

The brook becomes a gentle string,
As birds, they flutter, joyfully sing.
Amidst the trees, the echoes soar,
In harmony, we long for more.

The leaves compose a soft refrain,
A symphony of love and pain.
Each rustle speaks in silent tunes,
Beneath the light of silver moons.

As twilight drapes the world in peace,
The notes of nature never cease.
A song that calls us to believe,
In every breath, a dream conceived.

So hear the harp, its magic spun,
In forests deep, beneath the sun.
Let melodies of life imbue,
The quiet heart, forever true.

Radiant Treasures of the Hidden Grove

In forests deep where sunlight weaves,
Lie treasures hidden 'neath the leaves.
A world of wonder, soft and bright,
Awaits the seeker, keen in sight.

Gems of dew on petals rest,
Nature's bounty, truly blessed.
The vibrant blooms and whispered lore,
Invite the heart to seek for more.

Through tangled roots and shadows cast,
The beauty found will ever last.
In every corner, secrets lie,
In hues of green and azure sky.

The breeze unfolds a fragrant tale,
An ancient dance that will not pale.
In radiant hues, the petals gleam,
An endless echo of a dream.

So wander through the grove's embrace,
Where every sight is filled with grace.
What lies within, we'll come to know,
In radiant treasures, spirits glow.

The Veil of Surreal Flora

In gardens where the strange blooms grow,
A veil of flora puts on a show.
With petals spun in colors rare,
They whisper secrets, dark and fair.

In twilight's dance, the shadows blend,
A dreamlike realm where worlds transcend.
The vines entwine with soft allure,
In surreal grace, they beckon pure.

The flowers speak through gentle sighs,
In muted tones that mesmerize.
A space where time is lost, anew,
In every pulse, a hidden view.

So take a step through petals wide,
Embrace the magic deep inside.
In this surreal garden's sway,
The veil of flora guides our way.

Remember well the wonder found,
Where beauty blooms from solid ground.
In every leaf, a story calls,
Within the veil, enchantment falls.

Fables Beneath the Canopy

In shadows deep where secrets lie,
A whisper spreads, a gentle sigh.
The ancient trees, they hold the tale,
Of moonlit nights and stars that pale.

Creatures small with eyes so wide,
In forest realms where dreams abide.
Each fable spun from rustling leaves,
Weaves magic strong, and hope believes.

A fox darts quick through bramble's snare,
With cautious steps, a tale to share.
Beneath the canopy, hearts unite,
In laughter soft or silent fright.

As sunlight streams through branches green,
The air alive with wonders seen.
Each murmur tells of love, loss, gain,
Of joy that dances in the rain.

So wander deep and lose your way,
In stories bright, let spirits play.
For fables shared beneath the trees,
Will linger on with every breeze.

A Tapestry of Celestial Petals

In gardens vast where starlight weeps,
A tapestry of petals sleeps.
Colors bright like dreams unfurl,
Their fragrance hints of magic's swirl.

Whispers soft of nightingale,
In this realm, all hearts prevail.
Moonbeams play on velvet blooms,
While echoes chase away the glooms.

Each petal tells of skies above,
Of fleeting moments, loss, and love.
In silken hues, the stories blend,
As night transforms and days transcend.

With each dawn, the blossoms sway,
And welcome in the golden ray.
They dance to songs of nature's art,
A symphony that warms the heart.

So linger long where petals shine,
In every hue, a life divine.
A tapestry spun from the stars,
Awaits the world beyond its bars.

Hues of Imagination's Heart

In realms where dreams take flight and soar,
The hues of thought unlock each door.
From vibrant reds to calming blues,
A canvas blooms, a world that brews.

With brush of wind and stroke of light,
Imagination paints the night.
Each color holds a secret deep,
Awakening wonders from their sleep.

Golden yellows, whispers bright,
Illuminating the heart's delight.
Through every shade, a story flows,
In thoughts so wild, the spirit grows.

From pastel skies to shadows stark,
In every shade, resides a spark.
A journey starts with but a glance,
In hues that lead us to our dance.

So wander through this vivid realm,
Where dreams reside and thoughts overwhelm.
For in this heart of hues so pure,
Imagination's light shall endure.

Tales from the Enchanted Orchard

In orchards lush where fruits entwine,
Tales whisper soft, sweet, and divine.
Each apple glows with stories bold,
Of lovers lost and treasure untold.

The branches sway with ancient grace,
As echoes dance in time and space.
Beneath the boughs, the shadows play,
Inventing worlds where children stay.

A squirrel chats of sunny days,
Of gentle winds and sunlit rays.
With every bite of juicy treat,
A story blooms, both rich and sweet.

As twilight falls, the stars align,
The orchard holds a magic sign.
In every fruit, a dream is sown,
A tapestry of love and home.

So stroll the paths where tales are spun,
In every corner, laughter runs.
For in this orchard, hearts will find,
A haven where the soul's defined.

Soft Caress of the Cosmic Blooms

In twilight's embrace, petals unfold,
Whispers of starlight in hues of gold.
The night blooms gently, with scents that soar,
Each fragile heart opens, seeking more.

Dancing on winds from galaxies far,
Dreams weave their paths like threads in a star.
A melody plays beneath cosmic streams,
Carried on breezes that cradle our dreams.

Glimmers of magic in every sweet smile,
Soft caress of blossoms, delicate style.
The world fades away, lost in this spell,
Wrapped in the fragrance where wonders dwell.

Moonlight shines softly on every bloom's face,
Nature's kind secrets in this sacred space.
Together we wander through night's gentle weave,
In the soft caress, hearts learn to believe.

The Serpent's Laugh Among the Daisies

In meadows where daisies sway to and fro,
A serpent curls gently, moving so slow.
Its laughter like ripples in sunlight's warm glare,
Echoes of mischief in summer's sweet air.

With scales like the twilight, it shimmers and glows,
A trickster who dances where wild beauty grows.
Amidst golden blooms, a tale begins to spin,
Of secrets and whispers, of loss and of win.

Soft rustling sounds from the brush nearby,
The serpent's sly smile as it slithers on by.
Daisies stand tall, offering their cheer,
While laughter of shadows is all that we hear.

In a game of the sun and the shadows that play,
The serpent will chuckle, then slither away.
Leaving behind just the scent of sweet grass,
And the fleeting enchantment that moments surpass.

Underneath the Celestial Canopy

Beneath the vast heavens, where stars twinkle bright,
Mysteries whisper in the velvet night.
Gathered in silence, we breathe in the sky,
Underneath the canopy, where dreams drift by.

Constellations weave tales in patterns divine,
With each glimmering spark, our spirits entwine.
Voices of stardust dance soft through the air,
Carrying wishes to places laid bare.

The moon casts her glow, a guiding soft light,
While shadows of longing take flight in the night.
In this sacred haven, where hearts intertwine,
Underneath the celestial, magic we find.

In the hush of the cosmos, all sorrows dissolve,
Lost in the wonder that stars can involve.
Together we cherish the night's gentle beauty,
Underneath the celestial, we find our true duty.

Kaleidoscope of Mystic Flora

In a garden where colors collide and embrace,
Mystic flora awakens, a magical place.
Petals like rainbows, a vibrant display,
Spin tales of wonder in the light of the day.

Spirals of fragrance twist through the air,
Each blossom a story, unique and rare.
With roots deep in earth, and heads turned to sky,
These wonders of nature are never shy.

Butterflies flutter with wings of delight,
Kissing each petal, a wondrous sight.
A kaleidoscope dances in sunlight's sweet kiss,
Where time seems to linger in fragrant bliss.

In harmony swaying, each flower aligns,
Creating a symphony where beauty shines.
Mystic flora garden, a tapestry spun,
A world full of magic, where life has begun.

Echoes from the Moonlit Grove

Beneath the glow of silver light,
The whispers dance through tranquil night.
Each shadow plays a gentle tune,
In harmony with the soft, bright moon.

The ancient trees, with secrets low,
Breathe tales of love from long ago.
Their branches weave a mystic lace,
Embracing time in this hushed place.

A brook flows softly, crystal clear,
Its laughter echoes, sweet and near.
While fireflies twinkle, brief and bright,
Guiding lost souls in the night.

The air is thick with dreams untold,
Of brave adventures and heroes bold.
Here spirits dwell, both kind and wise,
Under the vast and starry skies.

So linger, if you dare to stay,
And let the magic lead your way.
For in this grove, where shadows roam,
The heart finds light, and calls it home.

Dreaming Among Starlit Petals

In gardens where the night blooms bright,
I weave my dreams in the soft twilight.
The petals whisper tales of old,
Of secrets wrapped in scents so bold.

The moonlight kisses every leaf,
While shadows weave their gentle grief.
Each flower sways with timeless grace,
A dance of whispers in this space.

With every sigh, the blooms unfold,
Like stories waiting to be told.
In colors rich, the heartbeats race,
In starlit glens, we find our place.

A breeze carries the sweetest song,
As night envelops the world along.
Each starlight spark a hope, a wish,
In every petal, dreams we cherish.

So linger here, where wonder grows,
And let the magic cradle woes.
For in this realm of softest light,
Our dreams take flight into the night.

The Garden Beyond Reality

Beyond the veil of time's cruel hand,
Lies a garden, vast and grand.
Where colors sing and shadows play,
And dreams weave paths in bright array.

Each flower holds a whispered truth,
A gateway back to lost sweet youth.
With every step on mystic ground,
The heart awakens, hope resounds.

The sunlight dances on the streams,
Where laughter merges with our dreams.
In harmony, the creatures sing,
And every joy the breezes bring.

The vines embrace the ancient stones,
While nature hums her cheerful tones.
Time bends here, breathing life anew,
Creating marvels just for you.

To wander through this wondrous place,
Is to find peace, a warm embrace.
For in this garden's gentle glow,
The heart learns more than we can know.

Secrets of the Glittering Glade

In the glade where fairies weave,
Ancient tales make hearts believe.
The sparkle of the dew at dawn,
Holds secrets of the magic drawn.

Each rustle in the emerald ferns,
Awakens dreams, our spirit yearns.
The air is thick with laughter's ring,
While the woodland whispers soft and sing.

Amidst the flowers, shadows flit,
A dance where time and light both sit.
In every hue, the stories meld,
Of lost loves found and dreams upheld.

The glow of dusk unveils the night,
As sparkles fade with waning light.
But in the heart, the glade remains,
A sanctuary where hope sustains.

So venture into this secret space,
And let the magic take its place.
For in the whispers of the glade,
A world of wonder shall not fade.

The Dance of Nebulous Petals

In twilight's hush, the petals sway,
A whispered tale of dusk's ballet.
They twirl in colors, soft and bright,
Beneath the watchful stars of night.

With every breeze, they weave their song,
In gardens where all dreams belong.
They shimmer like the cosmos' dream,
In nature's peaceful, sacred scheme.

Embraced by time, they spin and dive,
In fragrant waves, they dance alive.
A symphony of hue and grace,
Adrift in time's enchanting space.

Glistening Grasses of Otherworldly Realms

Where emerald blades meet silver light,
In realms unknown, so pure, so bright.
A carpet lush, where wishes tread,
With every step, sweet magic spread.

The dew-kissed tips, like diamonds rare,
Reflect the dawn's soft, golden glare.
In whispers soft, tales long untold,
In every blade, a spark of gold.

Among the shadows, secrets dwell,
In grassy waves, they bid farewell.
The breeze will carry fleeting dreams,
In this realm where wonder gleams.

Serenade of the Mystical Greenthumb

Beneath the moon, a garden grows,
Where every bloom and petal knows.
The touch of hands, both kind and wise,
Awakens magic 'neath the skies.

With tender heart and whispered cheer,
The greenthumb's song, so sweet to hear.
A lullaby of soil and seed,
In every plant, a heartfelt creed.

Through morning mist, their souls entwine,
In vibrant hues that brightly shine.
With every leaf, a story told,
Of love and life, of hope and gold.

Through Fields of Prism and Light

Through fields where colors blend and merge,
In rays of sunlight, all fears purge.
The blossoms burst, a radiant sight,
In harmony with day and night.

These vibrant lands, alive and free,
A canvas bright, for all to see.
In every shade, a memory lies,
Of whispered dreams and endless skies.

With every step, a journey starts,
In fields where nature's magic sparks.
With laughter spun in light's embrace,
We find our dreams in this sweet space.

Reverie of the Starlit Glade

Beneath the moon's soft, silver glow,
The whispers of the night do flow.
In glades where secrets seem to sigh,
The dreams of starlit hearts will fly.

Each leaf a tale, each breeze a song,
In night's embrace, we all belong.
With fireflies dancing in delight,
This magic cradle holds us tight.

Among the shadows, echoes call,
Where ancient wonders weave through all.
In reverie, we glimpse the past,
A tranquil moment, fading fast.

The glade adorned in twilight's wear,
Where hopes and sorrows blend and share.
With every heartbeat, stories churn,
In sacred space, our spirits yearn.

In whispers low, the stars convene,
Unfolding wonders yet unseen.
Beneath the branches, secrets swell,
In starlit glade, we find our spell.

Wandering Trails of Fabled Creatures

On paths where shadows intertwine,
The fables of old softly define.
Woodland whispers guide our feet,
Where royalty and magic meet.

Through emerald glens and misty veil,
The tales of creatures weave a trail.
With every rustle, heartbeats race,
In nature's arms, we find our place.

The pixies' dance, a delicate wisp,
An owl's wise gaze, a timeless lisp.
Each footprint tells a story grand,
Of fabled creatures from the land.

The forest breathes, alive and free,
With echoes of sweet tapestry.
We wander forth, enchanted, bold,
In search of legends yet untold.

When twilight falls, the magic stirs,
A symphony of sounds occurs.
In every turn, a spark ignites,
On wandering trails, our hearts take flight.

Blossoming in the Realm of Legends

In gardens where the lilies bloom,
The air is sweet with sips of gloom.
Each petal whispers stories old,
In fragrant breaths, their tales unfold.

The shadows dance beneath the trees,
While legends float upon the breeze.
In every color, life ignites,
A canvas filled with pure delights.

With every bud, a promise grows,
In silent verses, nature shows.
The secrets shared in softest sighs,
In blooming heart, our wonder lies.

In twilight's gaze, the magic swells,
Where dreams and legends weave their spells.
With every glance, a spark we find,
In realms of marvels intertwined.

In laughter soft, beneath the sun,
The blooming realms of tales begun.
Let nature's treasures guide our way,
In legend's grasp, we choose to stay.

Where Nature Meets the Unseen

Upon a hill where silence reigns,
The whispers echo through the plains.
In shimmers bright, the air is sweet,
Where nature's pulse and magic meet.

Among the trees where shadows wane,
The unseen lingers, whispers plain.
With every rustle, spirit gleams,
Residing in our softest dreams.

Through crystal streams and silver brooks,
The journey hides in ancient books.
Where flowers bloom in vibrant hues,
The unseen world brings forth its muse.

In moonlit nights, the magic stirs,
In quiet hearts, a knowledge purrs.
With each step taken, the veil lifts,
In twilight's grace, we find our gifts.

At nature's edge, we pause and breathe,
With open hearts, we dare believe.
In every sigh, the unseen sings,
Where love and truth embrace our wings.

Majestic Flora Under the Veil

In twilight's glow, the petals gleam,
Whispers of secrets in a luminous dream.
Beneath the arch of twilight's veil,
Nature's magic sings a wondrous tale.

Crimson and gold in brilliant hues,
Dancing softly in the gentle muse.
Bees hum sweetly, their work divine,
In the garden's heart, where wonders entwine.

A breeze of jasmine stirs the air,
Inviting all to linger and share.
Each leaf a story, each stem a rhyme,
In this blessed realm, untouched by time.

Moonlit nights bring a tender grace,
Where dreams and flowers find their place.
A world that breathes, where shadows play,
In majestic flora, magic won't sway.

So wander deep where the wild things roam,
In the heart of nature, you'll find your home.
For in every blossom, a secret drawn,
In this enchanted land, a new dawn.

Mystical Pastures of Serenity

In pastures lush, where silence reigns,
The gentle whisper of soft refrains.
Where daisies wink in the golden light,
And dreams take flight in the soft twilight.

A brook that giggles through stones so gray,
Offers a song to the close of day.
With every rustle of emerald grass,
Magic weaves through as moments pass.

Fairies flit on gossamer wings,
In secret corners, where the nightingale sings.
They weave their spells in the evening glow,
Crafting tales that the wildflowers know.

The sky blushing pink as the day departs,
Fills the heart with softening arts.
In this serene meadow, peace is found,
A sanctuary where dreams abound.

So come, embrace the tranquil embrace,
In mystical fields of endless grace.
With laughter and whispers in the tender air,
A gentle world beyond compare.

When Shadows Kiss the Wildflowers

When shadows dance 'neath the silver moon,
The wildflowers sway to a secret tune.
They scatter dreams in the nighttime air,
Whispering stories of moments rare.

A silver mist blankets the earth,
Cradling the blossoms of magical birth.
Every petal whispering soft and low,
In the tender grip of a twilight glow.

Moths flutter gently, drawn to the light,
Painting the darkness with colors bright.
In this realm of wonder, enchantments twine,
As shadows and flowers in harmony shine.

The wind carries secrets through branches high,
Awakening dreams like the stars in the sky.
In a moment of stillness, the heart knows why,
Nature's sweet symphony makes time fly.

So pause for a heartbeat, breathe in, and feel,
The magic alive beneath each flower's heel.
For in every shadow where wildflowers sway,
A world of enchantment forever will play.

The Blooming Haven of Fantasies

In a hidden nook where fantasies dwell,
Flowers bloom in a vibrant spell.
Petals shimmering in colors pure,
Inviting dreamers to explore and cure.

A canopy woven from leaves so bright,
Offers shelter in the heart of night.
With starry whispers that beckon near,
Carrying wonders for all who hear.

Butterflies dance in a jubilant whirl,
Painting the air in a bright swirl.
Their laughter echoes, sweet and clear,
In this blooming haven, cast aside fear.

The brook giggles softly, a crystal song,
In a symphony where all belong.
Every droplet a word, a secret spilled,
In a tapestry of dreams, endlessly filled.

So wander this grove, let your heart decide,
In the blooming haven, let magic be your guide.
For each step a story, a journey begun,
Where fantasy reigns, and the heart's never done.

Tales from the Sylvan Heart

In the glen where shadows play,
Whispers of the trees hold sway.
Secrets dance on winds so light,
As twilight paints the world in night.

Mushrooms twinkle, stars aglow,
Beneath the boughs, soft voices flow.
A melody of life unfolds,
In every leaf, a tale retold.

Foxes dart through dappled shade,
In this haven, dreams are made.
Moonbeams laugh on silver streams,
Weaving softly through our dreams.

The ancient oak stands proud and wise,
With branches reaching for the skies.
Each ring a story, each knot a truth,
Guarding the laughter of eternal youth.

Thus the sylvan heart beats strong,
In harmony with nature's song.
Through the ages, it will stay,
A timeless realm, come what may.

Whimsy Woven with Nature's Thread

In the meadows where daisies spin,
A tapestry of life begins.
Colors twirl like children's glee,
Nature's thread, wild and free.

Butterflies flit with gentle grace,
Painting smiles upon each face.
With laughter kissed by morning dew,
A world where dreams can all come true.

The sunbeams dance on golden fields,
Harvesting joy that nature yields.
Every whisper, every sound,
Weaves a magic all around.

With every petal, every leaf,
A story spun, a sweet belief.
In the heart of the vibrant glade,
Whimsy blossoms, never to fade.

In this realm where magic's found,
Life's enchantment knows no bound.
From humble soil, our hopes can soar,
In nature's arms forevermore.

Chronicles of the Celestial Grove

Beneath the arch of starlit skies,
A grove awaits where the heart flies.
Whispers of cosmos gently call,
In this embrace, we rise and fall.

Ancient roots entwined with fate,
As stardust sings, and spirits wait.
In moonlit glow, the night is bright,
Guiding wanderers with its light.

Each step unveils a woven tale,
Of dreams, of hope, where doubts turn pale.
Celestial winds caress the night,
Igniting souls with their pure light.

Through branches woven, secrets cling,
In each rustle, a memory sings.
The universe cradles every sigh,
As time hums soft, and spirits fly.

In this grove where wonders live,
The heart remembers to forgive.
Chronicles of the stars align,
In every bud, in every vine.

The Allure of Forgotten Gardens

In corners where the wildflowers bloom,
Secrets linger, dispelling gloom.
With ivy twined on weathered stone,
Whispers echo, once well-known.

Petals blush in radiant hues,
In the silence, stories fuse.
Amongst the vines, old dreams persist,
In every twist, a gentle mist.

The arches tremble with soft sighs,
As sunlight weaves its bright ties.
In shadows deep, the heart can roam,
Finding solace, feelings of home.

With every breeze, ghosts appear,
Memories fading, ever dear.
These gardens hold a timeless grace,
In forgotten paths, we find our place.

Embrace the layers, old and rare,
In the allure that lingers there.
For in each bloom, a heartbeat stays,
Through tangled roots and hidden ways.

The Radiance of Time-Worn Vistas

Amidst the hills where spirits dance,
The sunlight gleams, a fleeting glance.
Old oaks stand guard, their stories told,
In whispered winds, their secrets unfold.

Paths of wanderers, both young and wise,
Trace echoes of laughter beneath painted skies.
Each step a memory, each pause a dream,
In nature's canvas, time flows like a stream.

The twilight lingers with a gentle sigh,
As shadows stretch across the night sky.
Stars wink above like old friends near,
Holding magic within the silence we hear.

Through valleys deep where shadows sleep,
The stitching of dusk promises to keep.
Morning will come with its warm embrace,
Renewing the world in a brilliant grace.

Oh, radiance caught in the age's weave,
In every leaf, in every eve.
Nature's heart beats beneath our clime,
Echoes reverberate in the dance of time.

In the Shadow of Dreams and Petals

In gardens fair where fragrances dwell,
Soft petals whisper secrets to tell.
Each bloom a dream, a soft lullaby,
Bathed in the glow of the twilight sky.

Beneath the arch of the ancient trees,
Where sighs of the past float upon the breeze,
A tapestry woven with colors bright,
In the shadow of dreams, dance the night.

The path is kissed by the moon's soft weep,
In twilight's embrace, the world falls asleep.
Stars glimmer softly in a velvet dome,
In this sacred place, we find our home.

With laughter and whispers, the night takes flight,
Each petal a memory, a flicker of light.
In the shadow of dreams, we walk hand in hand,
With hearts intertwined in a mystical land.

As dawn begins to paint the earth anew,
Under the sun's warm and golden hue,
We gather the petals of dreams we've found,
In the garden where love and magic abound.

Colors Beneath the Whispering Breeze

In the meadows where wildflowers sway,
Colors burst forth in a joyful display.
Crimson and gold in a dance so free,
Beneath the soft touch of the whispering breeze.

The sun dips low, casting shadows long,
Nature's symphony sings a sweet song.
Winds carry stories from lands far and wide,
Binding the world where dreams coincide.

Each hue a promise, a tale to be told,
In the canvas of life, vibrant and bold.
Echoes of laughter, the flutter of wings,
In the heart of the meadow, the soul softly sings.

Through the rustling leaves, secrets take flight,
In the embrace of the soft moonlight.
Colors whisper softly, igniting our souls,
Filling the world with their dazzling roles.

So let us wander where wild things roam,
In nature's embrace, we find our home.
Beneath the vast skies, we dance with glee,
In the colors that flourish, wild and free.

Haven of the Gentle Blossoms

In a hidden nook where the soft winds play,
Gentle blossoms bloom in a sweet ballet.
Cradled in petals, whispering dreams,
A haven of peace where the sunlight beams.

Here time stands still in nature's embrace,
Each flower a smile, a tender grace.
The air draped in scents of honey and dew,
Where love's soft laughter drifts lightly through.

Beneath the branches where shadows blend,
The heart finds solace, a soothing friend.
In the rustle of leaves, the world calms down,
In the haven of blossoms, with joy, we drown.

With every petal that falls to the ground,
A story of love and life can be found.
Each moment cherished, each breath a song,
In this gentle haven where we belong.

So let us linger, let our worries cease,
In the garden of blossoms, we find our peace.
Where whispers of nature serenade the heart,
And the magic of stillness plays its part.

Secrets of the Fabled Pastures

In valleys deep where shadows play,
The whispers tell of times gone gray.
A breeze will carry ancient sighs,
From grassy knolls where silence lies.

Beneath the stars, the secrets weave,
A tapestry of dreams believe.
Each blade of grass, a story spun,
Of battles fought and victories won.

The moonlit nights, they softly gleam,
With echoes of a forgotten dream.
Where gentle hooves have trod the ground,
The pastures sing without a sound.

Among the flowers, wild and free,
The tales unfold like mysteries.
A fabled realm where legends roam,
In every corner, whispers home.

So wander far through emerald glades,
Where magic hides in sunlight's shades.
The secrets wait for hearts to seek,
In fabled pastures, lost and meek.

Ethereal Blooms in Twilight's Embrace

In twilight's glow, the petals sigh,
As colors bleed across the sky.
Each bloom aligns with stars above,
A dance of beauty, pure as love.

Beneath the arch of fading light,
The fragrant whispers take their flight.
In gardens kissed by night's caress,
Ethereal blooms, a soft finesse.

They shimmer gently, soft and fair,
With secrets held in evening air.
In twilight's grasp, their spirits soar,
While shadows linger, nevermore.

A symphony of fragrant dreams,
The starlit paths offer their themes.
With every petal, stories weave,
In twilight's grip, we dare believe.

So let us wander hand in hand,
Through fields of light, where hopes expand.
In ethereal blooms, we shall find,
The whispers of the heart entwined.

The Gallop of Mythic Gardens

In gardens lush where giants tread,
The tales of old begin to spread.
With every hoof that marks the ground,
The magic thrives in echoes found.

The gallop sings of distant lands,
Where time is painted by fair hands.
Each flower blushes, tales retold,
Of kings and queens, of brave and bold.

Through twisting paths of fragrant air,
The mythic blooms do softly share.
Their colors dance with vibrant glee,
In rhythms of eternity.

From lushest roots, the stories rise,
Like phoenix flames in dusky skies.
In gardens rich with lore profound,
The heartbeats echo all around.

So gallop forth, let spirits fly,
In mythic gardens, kiss the sky.
With every stride, the magic sings,
Of endless realms and wondrous things.

Lush Roots of Whimsy Untamed

In wild embrace where laughter grows,
The roots of whimsy twist and pose.
With every turn, a new delight,
In shadows deep, life ignites.

Each tiny sprout, a tale to share,
In tangled knolls beyond despair.
Through waves of green, the spirits play,
In luscious realms where dreams hold sway.

From ancient trees with laughter true,
A canopy where hope breaks through.
With colors vibrant, rich and bold,
The untamed stories dare be told.

So wander 'neath the arching trees,
Where every laugh rides on the breeze.
Embrace the whimsy, let it shine,
In roots entwined, your heart will find.

In wild abandon, join the dance,
Beneath the stars, take every chance.
For in the lushness, joy reclaimed,
Are roots of whimsy, forever untamed.

Hues of Enchantment Amidst Wildflower Tales

In fields where colors softly play,
A dance of blooms in bright array,
Whispers of magic fill the air,
Where tales of wonder hide with care.

The sun dips low, a golden crown,
Casting shadows, fading down,
Each petal holds a story grand,
In wildflower dreams across the land.

With dewdrops glistening like bright stars,
Nature weaves its soft memoirs,
A symphony of scents so sweet,
In every corner, magic meets.

Whispers of fairies on the breeze,
Amongst the blooms, the heart finds ease,
Each fluttered petal, soft and bold,
Shares secrets of the tales of old.

Beneath the vast and painted skies,
The wishful heart forever flies,
In hues enchanting, wild and free,
The world transforms in fantasy.

Celestial Canopies and Fantasy Vineyards

Under the sky, a tapestry bright,
Stars weave their stories in the night,
Vineyards stretch in rows divine,
Where dreams and grapes together twine.

The moonlight kisses every hue,
A whisper soft, of fables new,
Each vine a promise, rich and bold,
In rustic charm, the past unfolds.

Carriages glide on paths of gold,
With ancient stories yet untold,
Celestial canopies above,
A dance of starlight, time, and love.

In every sip, a tale takes flight,
Of summer days and tender nights,
With laughter shared beneath the leaves,
In every heart, the magic weaves.

The harvest sings in every breeze,
A joyful song through swaying trees,
Together we toast the skies above,
In vineyards blessed with dreams and love.

Tails of Lavender and Magic

In fields of lavender, dreams take root,
Where purple whispers softly shoot,
A fragrant tale upon the breeze,
Awakens hearts, a soul's sweet tease.

Each stem a secret, deep enchanting,
Where bees are busy, flowers dancing,
In twilight's glow, the magic flows,
Among the blooms, the wonder grows.

Petals like whispers, soft and light,
Share stories spun in the fading light,
A scented waltz beneath the moon,
As stars ignite the night's sweet tune.

The gentle hum of nature sings,
Of hidden tales and soft-spun things,
Every breeze carries soft delight,
In lavender dreams, we take to flight.

With smiles painted in hues so fair,
Magic rests in the evening air,
As hearts entwined with nature's art,
Find solace in the lavender's heart.

The Lure of the Mythic Horizon

Beyond the edge where skies collide,
Awaits a place where dreams abide,
The horizon calls with voices sweet,
A promise whispered, a journey fleet.

Mountains rise with secrets tall,
The echoing tales of those who fall,
Upon the path of the unknown,
In every heart, the fire has grown.

The waves embrace the sandy shore,
In ancient songs, the legends pour,
The lure of magic beckons near,
A world unseen, laced with cheer.

In every shadow, a quest awaits,
For curious souls and open gates,
The horizon, painted in dreams so bright,
Calls forth the brave to chase the light.

In twilight's glow, the journey starts,
With fire in eyes and hopeful hearts,
The mythic horizon whispers clear,
In every step, adventure near.

A Journey Through the Whispering Fields

In whispers soft, the breezes sing,
Among the blooms, new dreams take wing.
With every step, the stories flow,
In gentle hues, the secrets glow.

The path is lined with golden light,
Where shadows dance, and hearts take flight.
The flowers nod, a knowing glance,
Enticing all to join the dance.

Through fields of hope, my spirit roams,
In nature's arms, I find my home.
With every breeze, my worries cease,
And in this peace, I find release.

A symphony of rustling leaves,
In nature's voice, my heart believes.
The journey calls, a siren's tune,
Beneath the watchful, smiling moon.

Each step I take, the world unfolds,
In whispers deep, the truth beholds.
With open heart and open mind,
In these sweet fields, my soul will find.

Songs of the Dreamweaver's Meadow

In twilight's glow, the dreams begin,
With threads of light, the night wears thin.
Each note a whisper, soft and clear,
In melodies that draw me near.

The meadow hums a sacred song,
Where every heart, it does belong.
With every step, the visions dance,
Inviting souls to take a chance.

The stars above, like lanterns bright,
Guide weary hearts to find their light.
In shadows deep, the truth will bloom,
And banish all the depths of gloom.

Each moment holds a magic spark,
A journey forged from light and dark.
In whispered dreams, the past revives,
As long-lost hopes begin to thrive.

With every echo of the breeze,
I find a sense of sweet release.
The dreamweaver spins tales anew,
In this enchanted space, I grew.

In Harmony with the Blooms of Fate

In gardens rich where colors blend,
The blooms of fate, they twist and bend.
With gentle grace, they sway and sway,
In rhythms bold, they sing the day.

The petals whisper secrets bright,
In every shade, a spark of light.
With every breeze, their stories wend,
In fragrant paths, we find our friends.

Through petals' dance, our spirits soar,
In harmony, forevermore.
The world unfolds in vibrant hues,
In nature's hand, we chase our views.

In every bloom, a tale is spun,
A tapestry where we are one.
With every step, the journey calls,
Through fragrant dreams, the magic falls.

Together, we shall intertwine,
In blooms of fate, our paths align.
With every blossom, love will bloom,
In harmony, we find our room.

The Enigma of Wandering Petals

In twilight's haze, the petals stray,
With mystery, they drift away.
Each path they leave, a story told,
A journey fierce, yet soft, yet bold.

Through moonlit nights, their secrets weave,
In whispered tales, the soul believes.
In gardens lost and meadows wide,
The wandering blooms, they softly glide.

With every breeze, their essence flows,
A tapestry of tales that grows.
Among the stars, their laughter rings,
In companionship, the heart takes wings.

The enigma speaks in fragrant tones,
In every leaf, the past atones.
With every step upon the ground,
The petals' whispers can be found.

As dusk descends and shadows play,
I chase the petals, come what may.
In nature's grasp, I feel so free,
In wandering blooms, my heart will be.

The Spellbound Blossoms' Tale

In the glen where shadows dance,
A whisper floats on a twilight breeze.
Petals glow with a mystic glance,
Each bloom cradles ancient trees.

Woven spells in colors bright,
Charmed by moons with silvery beams.
They flutter soft in the fading light,
Guardians of enchanting dreams.

A secret kept in the heart of bloom,
Cloaked in the night's gentle sighs.
With every breeze, dispelling gloom,
They tell the tales of whispered lies.

Among the thickets, unseen friends,
Watch o'er magic that softly weaves.
Through time and space, their song transcends,
In the fabric of the world's eaves.

So wander ye near those hidden sprouts,
Where blossoms weave their story well.
In every petal, a tale that shouts,
The spellbound secrets they will tell.

Flowers of the Untamed Whispers

In meadows wild, the flowers sway,
With whispers bold, they sing of flight.
Each petal spins a tale of play,
In colors bright, a vivid sight.

Hidden paths where forests breathe,
Among the thorns, soft voices cry.
Untamed beauty, one must believe,
Throughout the night, beneath the sky.

Their roots entwined in ancient lore,
Where secrets waltz with morning dew.
Each bloom, a key to nature's door,
Unlocking worlds in myriad view.

Their laughter dances with the breeze,
A friendly chat amongst the trees.
With every sway, a gentle tease,
As they share the spells of ease.

So heed the call of petals bright,
They hold the dreams of earth entwined.
In whispered winds, they spark delight,
With magic tinted, pure and kind.

Verdant Visions at Dusk

As daylight fades with a gentle sigh,
The verdant leaves begin their show.
Underneath a canvas of grey sky,
Soft shadows stretch and quietly flow.

In twilight's hush, new dreams take flight,
The rustling grass, a soft serenade.
Nature's secrets hang by moonlight,
In every corner, magic's laid.

With each inhaled breath, a vision blooms,
Fruits of the earth, ripe and sweet.
In dusky warmth, the heart consumes,
Joyful tales that the night will greet.

Glistening dew on tender shoots,
Reflects the stars in soft embrace.
From silent roots to vibrant fruits,
Nature's hand paints every space.

So linger long in the deepening shade,
Let verdant visions cradle your mind.
For in the dusk, life's joys are made,
A tapestry of dreams entwined.

Fluttering Leaves of Serenity

In the calm embrace of morning light,
Leaves flutter softly, a gentle cheer.
Whispered tales take joyful flight,
In the essence of the atmosphere.

Each leaf tells of a summer's song,
Of breezes sweet that come and go.
In rustling whispers, they belong,
To nature's heart, an endless flow.

From tree to tree, they waltz and sway,
A harmony in every breath.
As daylight breaks, they greet the day,
In peaceful rhythms, life and death.

Swaying softly, a calming tune,
Their flutter brings a tranquil mind.
In the shadow of the silver moon,
Leaves of serenity intertwined.

So take a moment, feel the peace,
Let fluttering leaves guide your way.
In their embrace, find sweet release,
A world where worries fade away.

The Laughter of Wandering Buds

In the meadow where the wildflowers play,
Little buds whisper secrets of the day.
Tickled by breezes, their petals unfurl,
Giggling together, a colorful twirl.

Sunbeams cascade on their shimmering hues,
Painting the canvas with radiant views.
Each bloom a tale of joy and of grace,
Dancing in harmony, a bright, blooming space.

With laughter that echoes through thickets and trees,
They sway in the rhythm of soft summer's breeze.
As dusk gently falls, they twinkle like stars,
Celebrating moments, forgetting their scars.

In twilight's embrace, they whisper and dream,
Of adventures beyond, where magic does gleam.
Wandering buds that know freedom so true,
In this fragrant ballet, they flourish anew.

Ephemeral Touch of Nature's Kiss

Beneath the vast sky where the wild rivers flow,
Nature's soft touch helps the wonders to grow.
Glimmers of sunlight, like whispers so brief,
Bring forth the beauty, both magic and grief.

Petals awaken as dawn starts to blush,
In the hush of the morning, there's calm in the rush.
Each fleeting moment, like dew on the grass,
Illuminates secrets that shimmer and pass.

When shadows stretch long, and daylight will fade,
Every blossom remembers the journeys it made.
In the sighs of the night, there's a flicker of light,
A promise that life will return with the bright.

Through seasons that dance, in a cycle so fine,
Nature's soft kiss draws the heart into line.
Embrace the ephemeral, let go of the past,
For the glimpses of beauty are fleeting, yet vast.

The Quiet Rebellion of Blooming Dreams

In the still of the night where the shadows conspire,
Dreams linger softly, igniting their fire.
Each thought a seed, held close in the quiet,
Waiting for daylight, when they will riot.

The world seems asleep, yet beneath the slight earth,
Thousands of wishes hold promise and worth.
With whispers of courage, they push through the clay,
Defiant in spirit, they seek a new way.

In gardens of hope, where silence is loud,
Each tiny bloom rises, fierce and unbowed.
A rebellion of color, a stand against gray,
In the heart of the night, they celebrate day.

With petals like banners, they wave in the air,
A testament silent, a call to beware.
For every soft bud holds the dreams of the brave,
A reminder that beauty lies hidden and grave.

Cascading Ribbons in the Twilight

Across the horizon where twilight descends,
Ribbons of color begin to transcend.
Like flowing silk, they drape over the sky,
Whispers of magic as day says goodbye.

In hues of lavender, indigo, gold,
Mysteries beckon, enchanting and bold.
Each gentle hue tells a story once spun,
Reflecting the endings, embracing the sun.

With shadows that lengthen and stars that ignite,
The world holds its breath in the softening light.
Cascades of beauty in swirling embraces,
Painting the heavens with delicate traces.

As night softly whispers its dark, tender song,
Ribbons of twilight weave dreams all night long.
A tapestry woven from silence and sighs,
In the heart of the cosmos, where wonder still lies.

Through every transition, each rise and each fall,
Nature's own palette, a gift to us all.
So marvel in stillness when dusk is in play,
For light and dark dance in their magical way.

The Portal of Floral Fantasies

In gardens where the wild things grow,
A portal blooms, aglow with sunlight's flow.
Butterflies dance, with whispers soft and bright,
Dreams take flight in the embrace of light.

Petals paint the air with hues divine,
Each fragrance tells a tale, a sacred line.
Time stands still where the fairies weave,
In stories of the heart, we dare believe.

With every breeze, secrets gently twine,
A tapestry of souls, where stars align.
Through this gate of green and gold,
Adventures wait, in petals manifold.

The sun sets low, a golden crown of light,
As dusk invites the moon for its nightly flight.
In shadows deep, the magic stirs anew,
The portal glows, with wonders yet to view.

Mirrored Stems of Whimsy

In a realm where laughter sings,
Mirrored stems reflect the flapping wings.
Underneath the sky's vast dome,
Whimsy weaves a patchwork home.

Beneath the blooms, the stories sway,
Tales of joy from afar that play.
With every flicker, shadows cheer,
In this garden of dreams, we draw near.

Strawberries blush in the morning dew,
Where wishes hang on each petal's hue.
A world of wonder, bright and bold,
In every glance, a mystery unfolds.

Unicorns prance on paths of gold,
Through mirrored stems, their fate is told.
Dancing fairies spin tales in air,
As whimsy blooms in bustling flare.

Wind-Swept Tales of Splendor

Amidst the whispers of the trees,
Wind-swept tales flow with gentle ease.
The sky stretches wide, a canvas vast,
Where moments cling, yet swiftly pass.

In quiet corners, stories hide,
Of longing glances and hearts open wide.
The petals swirl in a twirling flight,
A dance of memories, sparkling bright.

With every gust, the echoes call,
From lovers' whispers to children's thrall.
In twilight's glow, the splendor gleams,
A tapestry spun from forgotten dreams.

Beneath the stars, on softest ground,
Legends of old in the breeze resound.
With each soft sigh, the night unfolds,
Wind-swept tales of splendor untold.

A Gossamer Path of Blooms

Along a gossamer path of dreams,
Where moonlight weaves through silver streams.
Petals blush, their colors bright,
In soft embrace of the gentle night.

In whispers low, the daisies sigh,
As fragrant secrets float and fly.
The path enchants, with every turn,
A world awakens, our hearts to learn.

Each blossom tells a tale of old,
Of treasures hidden and love retold.
On this journey, hand in hand,
We wander through a spellbound land.

The stars above, like diamonds twinkling,
Guide our hearts with their soft crinkling.
In every bloom, a magic glows,
A gossamer path where wonder flows.

Morning Dew on Mythic Greens

In dawn's embrace, the dew does glisten,
Whispers of secrets, the shadows listen.
Soft blades of grass, a jeweled sea,
Nature's canvas, wild and free.

Bright sun peeks through the leafy veil,
Guiding the heart on a timeless trail.
Each droplet holds a world untouched,
In quiet corners, dreams are clutched.

As morning stirs, the creatures yawn,
A symphony starts with every dawn.
In shimmering light, the day unfolds,
Stories of ages, now retold.

Glimmers of magic, soft and bright,
Enchanting souls with morning light.
With every step on this hallowed ground,
In nature's realm, pure joys are found.

So wander here where mythic greens,
Transform the mundane into splendid scenes.
Let the dew dance in the early sun,
In this sacred place, we are all one.

Whims of Nature's Palette

A splash of red on verdant ground,
Where colors clash and dreams are found.
Golden beams through branches sway,
Whims of color, night and day.

In the heart of woods, such hues collide,
Each petal's story, no need to hide.
The azure sky, a tranquil sea,
Whispering secrets only the leaves can see.

Emerald whispers dance with grace,
In Nature's palette, a sacred space.
Violet twilight trails the sun,
As every hue finds its way to run.

Soft breezes carry tactile shades,
In the stillness, the vibrant wades.
With strokes of light and dark entwined,
Artistry blooms, beautifully designed.

So breathe in deep the fragrant air,
Each color woven with utmost care.
Nature's whims, forever grand,
A masterpiece crafted by unseen hand.

The Splendor of Arcane Flora

Deep in the woods where shadows play,
Arcane blooms greet the light of day.
Petals soft as whispered lore,
Guardians of secrets from days of yore.

Draped in mist, the flowers sway,
In twilight glow, they softly stay.
Ferns unfold like ancient scrolls,
Revealing stories of hidden souls.

From twilight's maze, a fragrance blooms,
Enchanting hearts in nature's rooms.
With colors rich, they weave their spell,
In the breath of silence, the magic dwells.

Every stamen sings in tune,
With the rising sun, beneath the moon.
Each wondrous form holds a tale,
In whispers soft, they lovingly unveil.

So wander close where magics dwell,
In the splendor of flora, hear the bell.
A symphony sung by nature's hand,
In the heart of wonder, forever stand.

Where Dreams Intertwine with Grass

Beneath the stars, where dreams take flight,
The grass weaves tales of the night.
Soft whispers call the lost to roam,
In emerald fields, we find our home.

Each blade a thread in the fabric of fate,
Entwined with wishes, we patiently wait.
The moonlight dances on dewy tips,
As we sail on the night's gentle ships.

In dreams' embrace, where time stands still,
The heart's desires begin to fill.
With every sigh that stirs the air,
In the grass, our hopes are laid bare.

Amidst the starlight, laughter flows,
A tapestry woven from dreams that grows.
In nature's cradle, night's secrets hide,
As gentle breezes become our guide.

So lay your head on the earth so vast,
And weave your dreams with the night's soft cast.
Together we'll dance 'neath the twinkling skies,
Where dreams entwine, our spirits rise.

The Velvet Touch of Elfin Gardens

In twilight's hush, where shadows play,
The velvet touch of night holds sway.
With whispered dreams in starlit guise,
Elfin laughter lights the skies.

Beneath the moon's caress so bright,
Pixies dance in sheer delight.
They weave the air with shimmering thread,
Where gentle flowers rest their head.

Amidst the ferns and mossy glade,
The secrets of the earth are laid.
Each petal soft, with glimmering dew,
A world awaits, only for you.

With every step, the magic grows,
In this realm where pure love flows.
The velvet touch, a balm for souls,
Brings warmth to hearts and makes us whole.

So linger here, when day is done,
Beneath the stars, where dreams are spun.
For in the gardens, time stands still,
And whispers linger, hearts to fill.

Enchantment Amidst the Greenery

In emerald glades, where secrets weave,
The heart finds solace, learns to believe.
With each soft rustle of leaves above,
Comes the gentle touch of nature's love.

The fairies flit on wings of grace,
Painting smiles on every face.
They weave their magic, pure and bright,
Beneath the boughs, in soft twilight.

A brook sings sweetly, a silver thread,
Guiding wanderers where dreams are spread.
The scent of flowers fills the air,
Inviting all to linger there.

With every petal, every bloom,
Joy whispers softly, dispelling gloom.
In sunlight's dance on emerald blades,
Enchantment flourishes and never fades.

So take a breath, let worries cease,
In nature's arms, discover peace.
For in this place, where magic thrives,
The heart awakens, truly alive.

Blossoms in the Land of Reverie

In lands where dreams and petals blend,
The heart finds solace, hopes ascend.
Where blossoms swirl in gentle flight,
A tapestry of pure delight.

With colors bright, like painted skies,
Each flower holds a sweet surprise.
They whisper tales of love and light,
That dance in shadows of the night.

The breeze carries a fragrant song,
Entwining spirits, pure and strong.
Amidst the blooms, let worries fade,
In this haven, be unafraid.

With every step, the magic grows,
In time's embrace, the wonder flows.
Here in this land, with hearts set free,
You'll find the beauty meant to be.

So linger long, take in the view,
For in these blossoms, dreams come true.
In reverie, let your spirit soar,
And find the magic evermore.

Infinity Among the Petal's Embrace

In petals soft, where dreams reside,
Infinity blooms, where hearts abide.
Nature's whispers, sweet and low,
Guide us softly where love can grow.

With every breath, the beauty fills,
The air alive with joyous thrills.
Among the blooms, the soul takes flight,
Infinity in nature's light.

The colors dance in radiant hues,
Painting the earth with morning dews.
Each blossom tells a tale so grand,
In this enchanted, timeless land.

So close your eyes and feel the glow,
Let petals' magic gently flow.
In their embrace, find peace and grace,
Infinity found in this sweet place.

So wander forth, let worries cease,
In nature's arms, we find our peace.
For in each petal's soft embrace,
Infinity lives, our sacred space.

9 781805 620150